THE PURPOSE OF LIFE

Happiness that Transcends Old Age,
Sickness, and Death

THE PURPOSE OF LIFE

Happiness that Transcends Old Age, Sickness, and Death

Kentetsu Takamori

Translated and adapted by
Juliet Winters Carpenter

Ichimannendo Publishing, Inc.
Los Angeles   Tokyo

The Purpose of Life: Happiness that Transcends Old Age, Sickness, and Death
By Kentetsu Takamori
Published by Ichimannendo Publishing, Inc (IPI)
970 W. 190th Street, Suite 920, Torrance CA 90502
info@i-ipi.com
© 2024 by Kentetsu Takamori. All rights reserved.
Translated and adapted by Juliet Winters Carpenter.
All translations throughout this book, unless otherwise noted, are by Juliet Winters Carpenter.

NOTE TO THE READER:
Throughout this work, Japanese names are given in Western order. However, names of historical and literary figures who lived prior to Meiji era (before 1868) are given in traditional Japanese order, family name first.

Illustration by Hidekichi Shigemoto
Cover design by Kazumi Endo

First edition, November 2024
Printed in Japan

No part of this book may be reproduced in any form without permission from the publisher.

This book was originally published in Japanese by Ichimannendo Publishing under the title *Jinsei no mokuteki — Tabibito wa, mujin no koya de moko ni deau.* First edition: July 28, 2023.

Distributed in the United States and Canada by Ichimannendo Publishing, Inc. (IPI)
970 W. 190th Street, Suite 920, Torrance CA 90502
Distributed in Japan by Ichimannendo Publishing Co. Ltd.
2-4-20-5F Kanda-Ogawamachi, Chiyoda-ku, Tokyo 101-0052
Info@10000nen.com   www.10000nen.com

Library of Congress Control Number: 2024950201
ISBN 978-0-9601207-5-8

ISBN 978-4-86626-092-1

CONTENTS

CHAPTER 1 What Is My True Self?...................11

CHAPTER 2 What Does the Buddha's
Parable Signify? 37

1. The Solitary Traveler in a Wide,
Deserted Plain 38

2. The Bleached Bones Scattered
on the Plain 46

3. The Tiger in Hot Pursuit............................50

4. The Pine Tree at the Edge of the Cliff........59

5. The Slender Vine 64

6. The Traveler's Bind.................................67

7. The White Mouse and the Black Mouse.... 70

8. The Three Poisonous Dragons................... 72

9. The Raging Waters of a Bottomless Sea..... 78

10. Drops of Honey...................................... 107

CHAPTER 3 There Is a Light That Destroys the
Darkness of Despair...................... 115

AFTERWORD   Who Was the Buddha?............. 135

POSTSCRIPT Living on the Path of
No Hindrance 144

BIBLIOGRAPHY... 146

CHAPTER 1

What Is My True Self?

You Cannot Attain Happiness Without a Proper Understanding of Your True Self

The frontispiece of this book illustrates a parable that Śākyamuni Buddha told a crowd of listeners in India some 2,600 years ago. The parable is known today as "The True Nature of Human Existence." A traveler dangling from a slender vine over a raging sea: this image, the Buddha said, represents the plight of all humanity. Russian literary giant Leo Tolstoy—in seeking an answer to the question "What is a human being?"— came across this parable over two millennia later and declared in astonishment in his essay, "A Confession," "This is no fable but the literal incontestable truth which everyone may understand." Let us explore the parable that came as such a revelation to Tolstoy.

One day, King Prasenajit joined in the crowd assembled to hear the Buddha speak. Seeing him there for the first time, the Buddha gently began directing his remarks to the king: "Your Majesty, unless we begin with a proper understanding of who we are and what a human being is, we cannot know the purpose of life and attain happiness. So today, I will tell a story that illustrates the true plight of all human beings.

"Hundreds of millions of years ago, on a dreary evening when a chill wind blew, a traveler plodded alone across a vast, grassy plain. As he hurried homeward over the dimly lit pathway, he began to notice a scattering of white objects on the ground and wondered what they could be.

He stopped, picked one up, and realized in shock that it was a human bone. With no crematorium or graveyard nearby, why were so many human bones lying about? He froze and looked around uneasily.

"Soon, ahead of him he heard a fierce roar accompanied by rapid footfalls. He peered into the gloom and made out the figure of a tiger racing straight toward him. The meaning of the bones was instantly clear: these must be the remains of previous travelers whom the tiger had devoured. Now the same fate lay in store for him. The traveler spun around and tore frantically back the way he had come.

20   Chapter 1   What Is My True Self?

"At first he ran carrying on his back the money and possessions he had accumulated while working away from home, but in no time he cast it all to the ground. He ran and ran—but what human can outrun a tiger? The tiger came closer and closer. Soon the traveler felt the animal's hot breath at his back and knew he was done for. At the same time, he realized he must have taken a wrong turn, for the path ended abruptly in a steep cliff.

"Seeing his prey was trapped, the tiger surged confidently ahead.

The traveler spotted a tall pine tree growing at the edge of the cliff and, for a moment, thought he might escape by climbing it, but he gave up the idea since tigers can easily climb trees too. Then he saw a wisteria vine hanging over the edge of the cliff from one of the stout lower branches of the pine tree. In the nick of time, he grabbed hold of the vine and slid down to the end, relieved at his narrow escape.

"When he had caught his breath, the traveler looked up. The tiger stood at the edge of the cliff, growling in frustration. 'Thank goodness for this vine,' the traveler said to himself—and then looked down and let out a frenzied yell.

Directly below him were the raging waters of a bottomless sea, with high waves continually crashing against the base of the cliff. Between the waves were three poisonous dragons—one blue, one red, and one black—staring up at him with bright-red mouths wide open, just waiting for him to fall into their jaws. He trembled in horror and clutched the vine all the tighter. His situation was truly desperate.

"Yet fear, no matter how intense it may be, wanes over time like every other human emotion. As the traveler calmed down, telling himself that struggling would get him nowhere, he realized that he was famished and looked around for something to eat.

He glanced overhead and saw the most terrifying sight of all. Two mice, one white and one black, were circling the root of the vine, his lifeline, and gnawing at it by turns. If they kept it up, one of them was certain to bite through the vine and send him plummeting toward the ravenous dragons below. As his imminent peril sank in, the traveler turned chalky white, his teeth chattered, and he shook uncontrollably. But even that extremity of terror did not last long.

"Hoping to chase away the mice, the traveler yanked the vine, but the gnawing continued unchanged.

Every time he tugged on the vine, however, something dripped down. He reached out a tentative hand and discovered that it was honey. Honeybees had built a hive at the top of the vine, and by pulling on the vine, he had caused drops of honey to spill out.

The honey tasted so delicious to the starving traveler that it melted his insides. Captivated physically and mentally by the honey, he forgot about his peril and thought only of getting more and more honey to enjoy."

32   Chapter 1   What Is My True Self?

At this point in the story, King Prasenajit jumped to his feet in protest. "What a ghastly story! I can't listen anymore. Knowing what great peril he is in, how could the traveler be so intent on anything as trivial as honey? What a fool! It's too ridiculous to go on listening."

The Buddha said quietly, "Your Majesty, listen. The traveler is you."

"What? Why me?"

"Not only you. He represents everyone who has ever lived, in all times and places."

At these words, everyone in the crowd leaped up in astonishment. The Buddha waited for them to quiet down and then patiently began explaining the meaning of each part of the parable.

CHAPTER 2

What Does the Buddha's Parable Signify?

1

The Solitary Traveler in a Wide, Deserted Plain

The solitary traveler in a wide, deserted plain represents everyone who has ever lived, in all times and places. Many a song likens life to a journey. We are travelers journeying from yesterday to today, today to tomorrow. But along the way, the sun does not always shine. There are days of rain, wind, or snow, and there may also be hurricanes. The path goes sometimes up, sometimes down. Conditions on the journey of life are not always favorable. We experience sadness and pain, and at times we run into trouble.

What Is the Source of Our Aloneness?

Everyone's life journey is different, but all of us share one thing in common: we are all solitary and alone.

"That can't be right," you may say. "I've got parents and siblings, a spouse and kids, and a best friend too. I'm not all alone."

Physically, that may be true, but the Buddha taught that deep in each human heart is a secret storage place that the owner cannot reveal to anyone. That is why no matter how many people may be around, deep inside we feel a sense of solitude and loneliness. We are all truly "solitary travelers in a wide, deserted plain."

In the Larger Sutra of Infinite Life, the Buddha described our aloneness:

> Alone we are born and alone we die.
> Alone we depart and alone we come.

We are alone when we leave the womb and alone when we pass on. Everyone must come alone and depart alone. The Buddha taught that from beginning to end, human life means being alone.

Those Who Meet Must Part

In 1999, the brilliant Japanese intellectual Jun Eto committed suicide at the age of sixty-six. He was found collapsed at home less than a year after the death of his beloved wife, Keiko. His memoir *My Wife and I*, written out of his desire "to fully depict my wife's death and my crisis," is in effect his last testament.

> She murmured, "My life is over now. It's all finished."
>
> There was an echo of such profound desolation in her voice that I could make no reply. It came home to me then that everything was finished for me, too, and that there was nothing I could do about it. . . . Perhaps the medicine had brought her some relief, for she smiled peacefully, looked at me, and said, "We visited a lot of places together, didn't we?"
>
> "We certainly did," I said. "And each one was special in its own way." I could not bring myself to say the words, "We'll go again." Instead, tears running down my cheeks, I retreated into the kitchenette.

After his wife's passing, bereft of all purpose in life, Eto was left only with lonely hours of waiting for death.

> As long as my wife's life was not yet exhausted, down to the very last moment, I had the clear goal of staying with her and never leaving her alone; now that she is gone, I have no such goal. I am only obsessed body and soul with the coming hour of my own solitary demise, propelled second by second toward a meaningless death.[1]

This memoir, written with almost unbearable longing, caused a sensation. Two months before Eto committed suicide, author Yuichi Takai heard him say, "The nights aren't so bad, but being alone at home in the daytime is intolerable. When I can see every corner in the house, the emptiness hits me hard."

The Buddha taught that "those who meet must part." Every relationship, whether with a lover or a spouse, a parent or a child, a partner or a friend, begins with an encounter and ends in parting. And the day of our death, when we must part forever from all whom we love, will inevitably come.

1 Eto, *Tsuma to watashi*, 119–26.

The Loneliness of Being Ignored Is Hard to Bear

Having family around may lessen one's loneliness to a degree, but some studies show that the rate of elderly suicides is highest when three generations of a family live under one roof. Solitude is painful, but the loneliness of being ignored really hits home. The 1952 film *Ikiru*, directed by Akira Kurosawa, contains a scene that eloquently sets forth how it feels to be ignored by family.

Kanji Watanabe, chief of the Citizen's Section at Tokyo City Hall, takes time off work to consult a doctor about his severe stomach pains and learns that he has end-stage gastric cancer. Shaken and afraid of dying, he seeks comfort from his family, as anyone would do. His wife died early on, and Watanabe raised their son, the light of his life, single-handedly. He goes home and waits downstairs, planning to confide in him, but his son and daughter-in-law are out, and when they return, he overhears their conversation. His son wants to use his father's retirement money to build a new house for himself and his wife. In his shock and disappointment, Watanabe cannot bring himself to tell them of his diagnosis. The sound of cheerful music drifts down from the apartment upstairs, adding to his despair and loneliness.

Watanabe sits alone in the dark with his thoughts, reliving special memories: following behind his wife's hearse with his son, neither of them able to look away; cheering on his son at a baseball game; offering encouragement as his son is wheeled off to surgery. A deep tie of love once bound the two of them together, but now it is all a dream. Like a drowning man grasping at a straw, the father turned to his son for comfort, but his son was in a different world.

Eventually Watanabe cries himself to sleep under his blanket.

No Matter How Many People Surround Us, We Are Lonely Inside

Some readers may think that because they have an understanding life partner, a loving family, or a trusted friend of long standing, they are not lonely for now. But the Buddha taught that however trustworthy the people close to us may be, our souls are forever lonely and alone. No matter how many people surround us, we are lonely inside.

In 1927, before his suicide at age thirty-five, the short-story writer Ryunosuke Akutagawa said, "There are lots of people around, but I am lonesome."

We seek people who can understand us, and when we find them, we trust them and draw close to them. Yet can we fully open our hearts to our parents or children, our spouse, our friends? Everyone has a lonely core they cannot share with anyone.

The Buddha said that people all hide their loneliness and act lively, taking pains to distract themselves from their loneliness by traveling, eating good food, or enjoying music and art. They try to forget how lonely they are even a little by mingling in crowds at festivals and other events, but the effect is only temporary.

No matter what we do, we can never find lasting relief from our loneliness. That is because of the secret storage place inside us. As long as its door remains locked, once our temporary joy and pleasure are over, our loneliness will only intensify. The greater the pleasure, the greater the emptiness that comes afterward.

The Buddha likened human beings to travelers plodding alone across a wide plain, and he said that our solitary journey will continue indefinitely.

2

The Bleached Bones Scattered on the Plain

As he hurries homeward over the dim path, the traveler begins to notice a scattering of white objects on the ground and comes to a halt, wondering what they could be. He picks one up and realizes in shock that it is a human bone. His reaction parallels the shock we feel upon seeing or hearing of the sudden death of a friend or acquaintance. With news of the world instantly available via TV, radio, and the internet, we are bombarded with reports of deaths from war, terrorism, disasters, accidents, and disease. Such news from distant realms is apt to shock us far less than word of the death of someone close to us.

Must I, Too, End up as Bleached Bones?

The traveler picks up a bone off the ground in the evening twilight and, standing still, studies it quizzically. With no crematorium or graveyard nearby, why do so many human bones lie scattered about? He ponders the question and figures out that these must be the remains of travelers who passed this way before him. He shudders to think that one day he, too, will be reduced to bare bones. Then from far ahead he hears a strange roar, accompanied by fast-approaching footfalls. Peering into the gloom, he makes out the figure of a fierce tiger racing straight toward him. Instantly, all becomes clear: the bones are the remains of people whom the tiger devoured.

Exposed constantly to news of deaths in the media, we are like the traveler going through a field littered with the bones of others. The True Pure Land Buddhist monk Rennyo (1415–1499), in letters to his followers published later as *Gobunsho* (The Letters), vividly described the shock of learning of others' deaths: "People may have rosy faces in the morning but by evening turn into white ashes." Many families have seen off a smiling member in the morning only to break down in tears that evening at news of their loved one's passing. Rennyo continued as follows:

> Once the winds of impermanence have blown, our eyes are instantly closed, and our breath ceases for all time. Then our rosy color fades, and we lose our vibrant air. Family and relatives gather and mourn, to no avail. . . . They carry the body out to the fields for cremation, and after it has turned to midnight smoke, all that is left is white ashes. Words fail to describe the sadness of all this.

When he was nearly fifty, having seen so many bones scattered all around him, Tolstoy sensed the shadow of inevitable death. In "A Confession," he expressed his shock at this:

> I simply felt astonished that I had failed to realize this from the beginning. It had all been common knowledge for such a long time. Today or tomorrow, sickness and death will come (and they had already arrived) to those dear to me, and to myself, and nothing will remain other than the stench and the worms. Sooner or later

my deeds, whatever they may have been, will be forgotten and will no longer exist. What is all the fuss about then? How can a person carry on living and fail to perceive this? That is what is so astonishing! It is only possible to go on living while you are intoxicated with life; once sober it is impossible not to see that it is all a mere trick, and a stupid trick!

3

The Tiger in Hot Pursuit

The tiger represents impermanence, or mortality. That he is in hot pursuit signifies that death strikes suddenly.

Death is our universal destiny, but few people seem to give the matter much thought. The sudden passing of a relative, friend, or acquaintance forces us to stare the unpleasant fact of death in the face, which may cause us to tremble with anxiety and fear, but that is only a temporary state. Soon our minds are again full of whatever lies before us: work, relationships, illness or caregiving, parenting, financial problems, and so on.

Death Attacks Suddenly, from Behind

Even if we accept death as inevitable, we set it aside as something far in the future. Amid the busyness of daily life, we avoid all thought of our coming death. Yet all the while, the tiger is stealing closer, soon to pounce. Death is at once the universal fate of all humankind and an unwelcome visitor that arrives we know not when.

In the fourteenth-century classic *Essays in Idleness*, Buddhist monk Yoshida Kenko warned, "Death does not necessarily come from the front. It is ever pressing on us from behind." If we knew that death was sure to come from the front, we could prepare ourselves for its imminent arrival, but instead it sneaks up on us unnoticed, from behind.

The Buddha taught, "Death comes to old and young alike." In other words, there is no guarantee that the elderly will die first, followed by the young. If that were not true, young people could take satisfaction in thinking, "I still have a long way to go." But in fact, it is not unheard of for those in the prime of life to precede their elderly parents in death. All too often, young people and children lose their lives in natural disasters and accidents. Whatever their age, all people live side by side with death.

The late Hideo Kishimoto, a former professor of religion at the University of Tokyo, left a record of his ten-year battle with cancer in which he likened death to sudden, unprovoked violence:

> Death always comes suddenly. No matter when it appears, the one visited by Death looks on its arrival as a sudden intrusion. For the mind filled with a sense of security is totally unprepared for Death. ... Death comes when by rights it has no business coming. It goes coolly where, by rights, it has no business going, like a desperado striding with dirty boots into a freshly cleaned parlor. Death's behavior is outrageous. You may ask it to wait awhile, but in vain. Death is a monster beyond human power to budge or to hold in check.[2]

"I know I must die one day," we think, "but surely not tomorrow." When the next day comes, again we think,

---

2 Kishimoto, Hideo, *Shi o mitsumeru kokoro – Gan to tatakatta junenkan.*

"Not tomorrow," over and over again. Like someone unable to tread on his own shadow, we are unable to imagine that death may come as soon as tomorrow. Destined beyond any doubt for the grave, we go on blithely assuming we will never die.

Yet death strikes suddenly. "But my child is about to be married!" "But I want to watch my grandchild grow up!" "But I still have so much to do!" Without the slightest regard for our convenience, the pitiless tiger of mortality pounces all of a sudden.

Through the analogy of four kinds of horses, the Buddha distinguished four levels of sensitivity to one's own mortality:

1. Horses startled by the shadow of the whip.
2. Horses startled when the whip brushes fur.
3. Horses startled when the whip touches flesh.
4. Horses startled when the whip pierces bone.

The first type of horse gallops in fear at the mere glimpse of the rider's upraised whip. Such people are so sensitive to impermanence that the mere sight of smoke rising from a crematorium is enough to startle them into realizing their own peril. The second type of horse breaks into a gallop when the whip brushes its fur. People like this see the funeral procession or hearse of a total stranger and think in shock, "Someday it will be me." The third type of horse, surprised when the whip touches its flesh, represents those who contemplate their own death on encountering the funeral of someone they know: an acquaintance, relative, or neighbor. The fourth type of horse begins to gallop only when the whip has torn into its flesh and struck bone. This represents people whose first intimation of their own death comes on losing a loved one.

Which type of horse are we? Our degree of sensitivity to the shadow of death may differ, as the Buddha has pointed out, but surely the shock we all feel at news of others' deaths is the sign of a sudden awareness that we, too, must one day pass away.

Funerals Are Not Always for Others

Mount Toribe—
smoke was rising yesterday
and again today.
The people who pass by and see,
how long before their turn?

Mount Toribe, now located inside Kyoto city limits, was once the site of a crematorium. To paraphrase the anonymous poem above, people who pass by where yesterday smoke arose from the chimney glance at it and think, "Smoke again today. So many deaths!" The following day, smoke rises yet again. "Goodness, the deaths just keep coming," people think and pass on by. But those passersby themselves will not always be distant observers of others' ends. The day will surely come when others look on while their own remains are cremated.

As we get older, opportunities to attend funerals increase, but funerals are not always for others. The time is inexorably coming when other people will attend *our* funeral.

Today some people will die in automobile accidents. How many of them looked into the mirror as they brushed their teeth in the morning, grieving that this was their last day on earth? Sometimes after a morning like any other, the end comes suddenly.

"I'm ready to die anytime." "Dying is nothing." Some people glibly say such things, but one's own death is vastly different from others' and from what one imagines it will be.

It is said that a doctor with a terminal illness composed the following poem:

All this time it was
only other people who died,
or so I had assumed—
now the thought of my own death
is more than I can bear.

The difference between observing other people's deaths and contemplating one's own imminent demise has been likened to the difference between seeing a tiger in the zoo and coming face to face with one in the wild. The deaths of others correspond to looking at a caged tiger, not at one that sprang out of nowhere.

Paul Tillich, the German-born philosopher, wrote in his book *The Courage to Be* that human beings cannot bear even for an instant the "naked anxiety" of death. Fear of nuclear war, earthquakes, or climate change is based ultimately on the threat of death. A straight-on confrontation with death itself would be too terrifying, and so we concentrate on getting plenty of nutrition, exercise, and sleep; we schedule annual wellness visits; and we guard against natural disasters such as earthquakes and hurricanes, determined to escape the tiger of death.

In the parable, the traveler feels the tiger at his heels and casts aside all the money and treasure he worked hard to earn away from home.

After World War II, when television was just becoming popular in Japan, pro wrestling programs were all the rage. The pioneering wrestler Rikidozan felled international opponents with karate chops and became a world champion, to the delight of his compatriots. He acquired great wealth and bought extensive property in the United States. Once, flying over the continent with his wife, he looked down and bragged, "From there to there is all mine!"

Rikidozan died in his late thirties from stab wounds to the abdomen inflicted during a dustup in a Tokyo club. He reportedly begged the surgeon who attended to him after the incident, "Money is no object. Just don't let me die." Surely anyone faced with death would feel the same way. But Rikidozan's wish was not granted, and he died.

The traveler in Buddha's parable threw away all the money he had worked hard to earn and ran for his life—but no one can escape the ravenous tiger forever.

Some say that nuclear war or climate change will wipe out the human race. Even if those disasters can be averted, 150 years from now, everyone presently alive will be dead. Descendants of ours may somehow survive, but do we not need to face up with due solemnity to the fact that we ourselves will one day die?

Moment by moment, each of us is being pursued by the rapacious tiger. We may be mauled to death today or tomorrow. Even so, we live our lives blind to that reality.

4

The Pine Tree at the Edge of the Cliff

The traveler spots a tall pine tree growing at the edge of the cliff and, for a moment, thinks he might escape by climbing it, but he soon gives up the idea since tigers can easily climb trees.

The pine tree represents things we usually rely on, such as family, possessions, money, health, abilities, and social status. All are important in life, but being blessed with them does not allow us to escape the specter of death. The Buddha hinted at this truth by telling another story.

◆　◆　◆

A rich man had three wives. He doted on the first wife and catered to all her wishes, making her warm if she was cold and cooling her off if she was hot. Thanks to him, she lived in utmost luxury and was never out of sorts. Though less fond of the second wife, he had gone to great lengths to win her, even fighting off other suitors, so he kept her always at his side and made sure she never strayed. Wife number three he loved just to the extent that he summoned her when he felt lonely, sad, or troubled.

Eventually the man developed an incurable disease and took to his bed. Trembling in fear at the thought of his approaching death, he sent for his first wife, confessed how lonely he felt, and asked her to accompany him on his journey to the next world. She said bluntly, "Accompanying you in death is the one thing I cannot do."

This curt response left the man deeply wounded. He felt as if he had been pushed into an abyss of despair. But his unbearable loneliness made him decide to swallow his pride and ask the same favor of his second wife. Her answer was no less cold: "Your first wife, the one you are so crazy about, turned you down, didn't she? Well, I'm not interested either. You chose me, but I never chose you."

Nervously, the man appealed to his third wife, but to his surprise, she also turned him down. "I can never forget how good you have been to me, so I will go with you as far as the edge of the village," she said, "but that's the best I can do. After that, you're on your own."

In the End, Abandoned by All, We Must Set out Alone on the Mountain Road of Death

What lesson did the Buddha teach through this story? Let us break down what it means. The first wife represents the body. The moment we expire, we separate from our body on our deathbed. The second wife represents wealth and possessions, which we must leave behind when the funeral procession begins. The third wife represents our family, relatives, and friends. They can accompany us to the graveyard but no farther.

"If I take care of myself, I can live a long and happy life." "As long as I have money and possessions, I won't need to worry about the necessities of life." "Even if I fall ill, my family will look after me, so I'll be all right." In this way, we seek to reassure ourselves, making provisions to guard against calamity. Yet however robust our health, however great our fame and fortune, however loving our family and friends, in the end, abandoned by all, we must each set out alone on the mountain road of death.

> All of the treasure
> that I gathered in a dream
> now I leave behind;
> shouldering my karma load
> I set off all alone.

Life is indeed a dream. We accumulate many things, thinking "I must have that! And that!" But in the end we leave it all and die alone, taking with us only the evil karma we acquired in the process of accumulation.

The traveler was right in deciding to give up climbing the tree, which represents all we rely on in life. Clinging to it wouldn't have helped him escape the tiger anyway.

5

The Slender Vine

The traveler sees a wisteria vine hanging over the edge of the cliff from one of the stout lower branches of the pine tree. In the nick of time, he grabs hold of the vine and slides down to the end.

The slender vine to which the traveler precariously clings represents our short lifespan. The Buddha likened the human lifespan not to a stout wire rope but to an extremely narrow wisteria vine that could snap at any moment.

Thanks to medical advances, the average human lifespan has continually grown, but even so, few people live past one hundred. Compared to trees that live for thousands of years or the age of our planet, said to be 4.6 billion years old, one hundred years is but a moment in time.

Twenty years from now may seem like a long time ahead, but many people would agree that the past twenty years went by in a flash. In the end, even a life of eighty years feels all too short.

The Keener Your Sense of the Brevity of Life, the More You Will Live a Life Worthy of a Human Being

The Buddha once asked three ascetics to tell him the length of human life. The first ascetic said, "Five or six days." The second ascetic disagreed: "No, not five or six days. About as long as it takes to eat a meal." The third ascetic said, "Oh, no. Human life is shorter than the time it takes to take a breath."

The Buddha was greatly pleased by the last answer. "That's right. Just as you say, life ends before the breath that enters is exhaled. The keener your sense of the brevity of life, the more you will live a life worthy of a human being."

The Buddha went on to tell this parable: "Imagine there are four master archers here. They each shoot an arrow at the same time into the four directions: one to the east, one to the west, one to the south, and one to the north. The arrows fly at lightning speed. Now imagine that at the same time, a fleet-footed man starts running and catches all four arrows in midflight. I'm sure you will agree that such a man is very fast indeed. But what is even faster, what disappears before you know it, is human life."

There is no way for any of us to know when our life may end, but sooner or later the vine of life will break. For all any of us know, our vine may be extremely fragile and on the point of giving way at any moment.

6

The Traveler's Bind

"Thank goodness for this vine," the traveler says to himself—and then looks down and screams. Directly below are the raging waters of a bottomless sea, with high waves continually crashing against the base of the cliff. Between the high waves are three poisonous dragons—a blue one, a red one, and a black one—their bright-red mouths wide open, just waiting for him to fall into their jaws. In horror, he shudders and clings tighter to the vine. His situation is truly desperate. Yet despite the extremity of his situation, his terror does not last.

Fear of Any Kind Eventually Fades

No matter how terrified a person may be, their fear eventually wanes. Even the most intense emotions fade after a time. We might delight at having passed our exams, rejoice over marrying our sweetheart, mourn the loss of a beloved child, or sink into despair after losing our home in a fire, but no such feeling lasts forever, and our attention soon turns elsewhere. This is what happened to the traveler as well.

As the traveler calms down, telling himself that struggling will get him nowhere, he realizes that he is famished and looks around for something to eat. He glances overhead and sees the most terrifying sight of all. Two mice, one white and one black, are circling the root of the vine and gnawing at it in turns. As we know, the vine is the traveler's lifeline. If the mice keep on as they are, one of them is certain to bite through the vine and send the traveler plummeting toward the ravenous dragons below. Forgetting how famished he is, the traveler becomes obsessed with chasing away the mice.

He shakes the vine hard, but the pace of the mice's gnawing does not change. Rather, he finds that every time he tugs on the vine, something drips down. He tentatively reaches out a hand and discovers that it is honey. Honeybees have built a hive at the top of the vine, and his pulling on the vine caused drops of honey to spill out. The honey tastes so delicious to the starving traveler that he swoons. Captivated physically and mentally by the honey, he forgets about the various kinds of peril he is in and focuses solely on how to get more of the delicious food. He is utterly unable to think of anything else.

7

The White Mouse and the Black Mouse

The traveler thanks his stars for the vine and calms down a bit, but soon he is astonished to see a black mouse and a white mouse circling the base of the wisteria vine and gnawing on it by turns. What does this part of the parable represent?

Day and Night Take Turns Shortening Our Lives

The white mouse represents day, the black mouse night. Their circling the vine and gnawing on it represents the cycle of day and night shortening our lives. The mice never take winter or summer vacations but just keep on gnawing steadily away.

The effects of this gradual eroding of the narrow vine to which we cling can be seen in all sorts of ways. Our vision clouds, we grow hard of hearing, our teeth fall out, our faces grow lined and wrinkled, our hair turns gray, we grow stooped with age, our hands tremble, our legs wobble . . . in all sorts of ways, our bodies begin to fail us.

Which mouse will gnaw through the vine? Those who die in the day had their vine gnawed through by the white mouse; those who die at night had theirs gnawed through by the black mouse. In the end, every vine will succumb to one mouse or the other. Even now, the mice are going ceaselessly around and around our slender vines, gnawing and wearing them away until the inevitable day when one mouse, the black one or the white one, gnaws through.

8

The Three Poisonous Dragons

Below the feet of the traveler dangling from the narrow vine are three poisonous dragons—a blue one, a red one, and a black one—their bright-red mouths wide open, waiting for him to fall.

The Human Mind Contains
Three Toxic Worldly Passions

The three dragons represent the three worldly passions constantly churning in our minds.

The Buddha taught that each human being possesses 108 worldly passions, attributes that torment us and cause us to do evil. Of these, the three that trouble and torment us the most are desire, anger, and ignorance. These three worldly passions that daily cause humans to do evil deeds contain deadly poison and are known as the *three toxic worldly passions*.

The mind constantly thinks evil
The mouth constantly speaks evil
The body constantly does evil
Never has there been a single good deed.
                    (Larger Sutra of Infinite Life)

The Buddha mentions the invisible mind first, ahead of the mouth and the body, both of which show outwardly. This is because he always placed greatest importance on the workings of the mind. The mouth does not speak unless commanded by the mind. The body does not move in opposition to the mind. The actions of the mouth and body are all in the control of the mind.

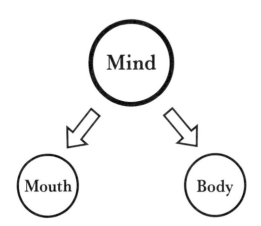

The mouth and body act
based on commands from the mind.

Criminal acts involve perpetrators and masterminds, those who direct the operation. The mastermind is the source of the problem. As the one directing and managing the crime, the mastermind naturally faces more serious charges. It would be rare indeed for the perpetrator to be charged with a felony and the mastermind to be found not guilty and acquitted.

The mouth and the body are perpetrators whose actions are directed by the mind.

Sparks fly up from a fire. The mind is comparable to the origin of a fire, and the actions of the mouth and body are comparable to flying sparks. Firefighters focus their efforts on the fire's origin. Actions of the mouth and body are expressions of the mind, so it is perfectly natural that the teachings of Buddha continually emphasize the human mind.

The Buddha pointed out that our minds contain three toxic worldly passions, and he likened them to three poisonous dragons. The mind of desire is likened to a blue dragon, the mind of anger to a red dragon, and the mind of ignorance to a black dragon. Let us take a closer look.

We Suffer at the Mercy of Our Endless Desires

We crave what we lack, and once we have it, we only want more and more. It is the nature of desire to deepen continually. Blue is also the color of the sea, and the deeper the sea, the more intense its hue; perhaps this is why the Buddha linked *desire* with the color blue.

Look around you, and marvel at all the people everywhere who suffer from uncontrollable desire and so create trouble for themselves and others. When we finite humans attempt to satisfy our infinite desire, we succeed only in destroying ourselves and placing enormous burdens on others. When we are free of stress, we can be considerate of others, but when we are cornered, our greedy, grasping nature bursts through. We become coldhearted, downplaying others' needs and thinking only of our own benefit. The many crimes that plague society spring from just such ruthless desire.

When Desire Is Thwarted, Rage Flares Up

"He humiliated me." "She cost me a fortune." We burn with fiery resentment. Our blood boils, and we grow red in the face; perhaps this is why the Buddha chose the red dragon to represent anger—the destructive mind that flares up within us when someone thwarts our desire.

"Anger begins in folly and ends in repentance," said Pythagoras. Anger burns up everything in its path and leaves you standing alone in burned-out ruins.

Anger makes us say things we should not, wounding others and filling us with regret and chagrin.

The Mind of Ignorance

The third dragon represents the ugliness of the mind of ignorance, also known as the mind of envy, jealousy, and resentment.

We envy those who outdo us. Anyone who surpasses us in talent or looks, wealth or possessions, fame or status, arouses our ire. When a rival gets the spotlight, we don't take kindly to it. And when someone we know suffers hardship, somewhere inside do we not feel a sense of relief even as we offer words of comfort? "The misery of others tastes as sweet as honey," goes a Japanese saying. Schadenfreude, the experience of pleasure at the misfortune of others, is indeed a universal emotion.

The Buddha may have likened this ugly emotion to a black poisonous dragon because it springs from pitch-dark ignorance—ignorance of the law of cause and effect.

If it were possible to project our innermost thoughts on a screen, would we want to show them to those we love? Pretty things, things we are proud of, we naturally want to show off. We can't wait to show others a new car, fashionable new clothes, or a new house. But nobody wants to show off a dirty room. The three poisons of desire, anger, and ignorance are constantly seething in the human heart.

One can only admire the Buddha's likening our mind of fearsome desire, anger, and ignorance to three poisonous dragons. The dragons in turn give birth to the raging waters of a bottomless sea. What does that sea represent?

The Raging Waters
of a Bottomless Sea

Below the feet of the traveler dangling from the end of the wisteria vine are the raging waters of a bottomless sea. Stunned to realize that the moment one of the mice succeeds in gnawing through the vine, he will plummet into the raging sea below, the traveler begins shaking uncontrollably.

Here it is necessary to have a clear understanding of the connection between the three dragons, the raging sea, and the three toxic worldly passions. Through this parable, Buddha taught that the sea and the dragons alike are the products of our three toxic worldly passions. The sea is the creation of desire, anger, and ignorance.

The Good That I Do Bears Good Fruits for Me; the Evil That I Do Bears Evil Fruits for Me

We must clarify the bedrock of the Buddha's teaching throughout his eighty years on this earth. That bedrock is the law of cause and effect, which has three elements: good actions bring good results, bad actions bring bad results, and your own actions bring your own results. In other words, the good actions you take bring about good results for you, and the bad actions you take bring about bad results for you.

The Buddha also taught that our lives extend across the three worlds of the past, present, and future, from trillions of years ago into the unending future. Because the law of cause and effect penetrates the three worlds, it is also known as *the law of cause and effect of the three worlds.*

> ### THE LAW OF CAUSE AND EFFECT
>
> ## Good causes produce good effects
> Good causes (deeds) produce good effects (happiness, joy)
>
> ## Bad causes produce bad effects
> Bad causes (deeds) produce bad effects (unhappiness, suffering)
>
> ## Own causes produce own effects
> Own causes (deeds) produce own effects (results)

Fish swimming in the swift current of a great river have no idea that they are in a great river. Just as fish cannot see the whole river in which they swim, we human beings, knowing only the present world, cannot tell that our lives extend from time immemorial into the future, through all eternity. Even so, it is true, the Buddha taught.

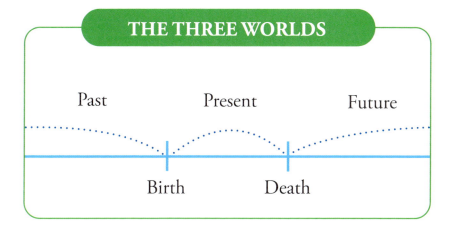

The three toxic worldly passions of which the Buddha spoke exist not only in the present world but throughout the three worlds. He divided the evil brought about by those passions into these ten categories: desire, anger, ignorance, frivolous speech, divisive speech, harsh speech, false speech, killing, stealing, and sexual misconduct.

Because of the three toxic worldly passions, our minds create evil so horrible that we could never speak of it to anyone. When that mind is expressed through the mouth, the result is frivolous speech, divisive speech, harsh speech, and false speech; when it is expressed through the body, the result is killing, stealing, and sexual misconduct.

82 Chapter 2-9 The Raging Waters of a Bottomless Sea

THE TEN EVILS

Mind:

Desire, anger, ignorance

Mouth:

Frivolous speech, divisive speech, harsh speech, false speech

Body:

Killing, stealing, sexual misconduct

Each of Us Has Wounded Countless People with the Keen Sword of Our Words

First, let us consider the evil actions of the mouth. *Frivolous speech* refers to empty compliments and arrogant, contemptuous words. *Divisive speech*, also known as *duplicity* or having a double tongue, is used to drive a wedge between people on friendly terms with each other and gleefully cut both sides to ribbons, out of jealousy. *Harsh speech* means flinging unfounded accusations at those you don't like, riding roughshod over them to get ahead. The last evil action of the mouth is *false speech*, which means taking pleasure in telling lies about others and deriding them.

The tongue is often likened to a sword. Who knows how many people each of us has wounded and made suffer with the words our tongue has spoken? Even if you say something harmful to someone without realizing it, the other person will remember those words with pain and bitterness till their dying day. Our careless words have wounded countless others, more than we will ever know. Words can even kill.

It Is Impossible to Live without Taking Life

Next let us consider evil actions of the body. Of the three mentioned by Buddha—killing, stealing, and sexual misconduct—we will focus on killing.

We think it is perfectly natural to kill and eat living things, but the living things themselves surely have a different perspective. Large or small, no creature wants to die. The reason freshly caught fish flop around on the deck of a fishing boat is because they are trying hard to stay alive.

Movies and manga occasionally portray man-eating monsters or giants. What if there really were a monster who needed human flesh to live? Who among us would willingly offer up our body for food? If we saw the monster consuming our parents or children with gusto, smacking its lips, would we not seethe with hatred?

The Buddha taught that all life is equal; none is higher or lower than any other. For human beings to value only human life is the height of arrogance. Since humans make the laws, no one is punished for eating animals raised for food, but the taking of life is still a dreadful act of evil. You may think that killing animals for food is all right since we do it to sustain life, but the Buddha, who always spoke the truth, clearly taught that it is evil.

"Yes, I eat meat and fish, but I'm not the one who does the killing." Some people may justify their actions this way, but it is precisely because there are people who enjoy meat and fish that producers of these foods engage in killing. Since in effect we commission them to do the killing for us and then dine with relish on the meat and fish they supply, the Buddha taught that we share in their sin.

"I'm a vegan. I don't eat or use animal products," some may say. But many vegetable farms do rely heavily on pesticides. Pests like mosquitoes, flies, and cockroaches, moreover, are often killed without a moment's thought. And who can say how many tiny lives we crush to death just by walking down the road? The sin of killing is everywhere and unavoidable.

Destruction of the environment through deforestation and through global warming caused by carbon dioxide emissions kills untold numbers of living things. The convenience we enjoy exacts a heavy toll. None of us can live without committing the sin of killing.

Was Urashima Taro Truly Kindhearted?

In a Japanese folk tale, a young fisherman named Urashima Taro saves a sea turtle from being tormented by children and is rewarded with a trip to the undersea Dragon Palace, where he is royally entertained. When he returns home, he feels lonely and opens the jeweled box he was given, only to turn instantly into a white-haired old man.

Once when a Japanese speaker introduced this folk tale at an overseas event, his audience reacted with puzzlement. "What's the moral of the story?" they asked. "Does it mean we shouldn't interfere when animals are teased? Is it warning us to beware of beautiful women like Princess Otohime?" He found their reaction surprising. The tale is traditionally taken to mean that we, like Urashima Taro, should be kind to animals. Yet there is a deeper meaning that is often overlooked.

This is how the story goes.

◆　◆　◆

One day, a fisherman named Urashima Taro sets out to go fishing. On the beach, he sees a crowd of children tormenting a big sea turtle. He takes pity on the animal and tells the children over and over to leave it alone, but they won't listen. The kindhearted fisherman then buys the sea turtle from them, takes it out to sea in his boat, and sets it free. The sea turtle thanks him profusely before disappearing underwater. Several days later, as Urashima Taro is fishing in his boat, up pops the sea turtle he rescued.

"To repay you for your recent kindness, today allow me to escort you somewhere nice." He takes Taro to the Dragon Palace at the bottom of the sea, where the lovely Princess Otohime entertains him with all manner of fine foods, and he has a wonderful time. When he eventually returns home and opens the jeweled box she gave him in parting, a cloud of white smoke rises, and instantly Urashima Taro is transformed into a white-haired old man.

◆　◆　◆

Can We Really Say That Urashima Taro is a Kindhearted Lover of Animals?

His coming to the aid of the sea turtle might have been a fine act of mercy, but don't forget that he carried a fishing pole over his shoulder. He had already taken the lives of countless fish with his pole and would continue to do so. You may well ask, "How can such a person be called a compassionate lover of animals?"

Urashima Taro is of course no criminal; he has broken no law. From an ethical and moral standpoint, he is a man of virtue. But the Buddha, who portrayed the true nature of human beings without regard for our convenience, taught that each of us is genuinely evil. We cannot avoid creating evil in our lives. Even if the evil is done to sustain life, like Urashima Taro's fishing, whoever commits evil must suffer the consequences.

Human life is spent creating evil unawares and passes by in the blink of an eye, so that all too soon one is aged and alone: perhaps that unflinching portrait is the real message of the story of Urashima Taro.

Is It Strange to Say That All People Are Evildoers?

Once, an elementary school principal came to hear a Buddhist monk preach a sermon. Buddha's teaching that all people are evildoers had always struck him as strange, and he had been waiting for an eminent monk to come along so that he might challenge him on that point.

The monk, having no idea what was on the principal's mind, began his sermon as usual: "In the eyes of the Buddha, there are no good people on earth. All are evil."

When the sermon was over, the principal went straight to the monk's chamber and said, "Just now, you said that all people are evil, but some are good, are they not? Otherwise, even schoolteachers would be evil, and the system of education would collapse. I trust you will choose your words more carefully from now on." Having voiced his complaint, he started to leave.

The monk swiftly bowed in humility. "I beg your pardon, sensei. I was unaware that someone of your high standing had come to hear my sermon. Please forgive me."

The principal was embarrassed. "Yes, yes. Just make sure you don't ever preach a sermon like that again." He hurried out of the room.

The monk followed him to the entryway and said, "Sensei, may I ask you one thing?"

"What is it?"

"Just now you said there are both evil and good people in the world."

"Yes, what of it?"

"I have a question I would like very much to ask you. Are you yourself good or evil?"

After all he had said, the principal could hardly identify with evil, and yet the idea of calling himself good made him uncomfortable. He was unable to come up with an answer.

"I'm not asking about anyone else," said the monk, "but about you yourself. Tell me this. Do you teach your young charges that lying is good or bad?"

"Lying leads to stealing, so of course I tell them it's bad."

"Then I take it you yourself have never told a lie?"

Everyone, not just the principal, can think of times in their life when they have lied.

"What about quarreling?" asked the monk. "Do you teach them that it's good or bad?"

"Naturally, it's bad."

"Have you never quarreled with your wife?"

Here again, marital spats are a near-daily occurrence in every marriage.

"Do you teach children that it is good to take life or evil?"

"Killing is evil. That goes without saying."

"So you yourself refrain from all killing?"

"No, I uh . . ." the principal said lamely.

"Then you yourself, while knowing lying, quarreling, and killing to be bad, lie, quarrel, and kill day in and day out. Yes?"

As the monk pointed out the various ways in which the principal was committing evil in his daily life without being aware of it, the principal began to show signs of reflection. Soon he sank to the floor and apologized deeply. "The more I think on it, the more I realize I can't begin to count up all the evil I have committed in my life without knowing. I beg you to forgive my earlier impertinence."

From then on, the principal listened earnestly to the teachings of the Buddha.

There is a vast difference between someone guilty of wrongdoing in the eyes of the law, someone guilty of wrongdoing from a moral or ethical standpoint, and the evildoer in the eye of the Buddha. The difference can be likened to the difference between the naked eye, a magnifying glass, and an electron microscope.

The palm of a hand seen by the naked eye or through a magnifying glass bears little resemblance to the same hand seen through an electron microscope. A hand that appears clean to the naked eye might prove to be quite soiled when seen through a magnifying glass, while the view through an electron microscope would reveal a shocking swarm of viruses and bacteria.

Laws created by human beings are the equivalent of the naked eye, while evaluations from an ethical or moral perspective are like a magnifying glass. And the Buddha's mirror, which shows us our true selves with matchless accuracy, corresponds to an electron microscope.

The actions of Urashima Taro are good, judged by the standards of the law, ethics, and morals, but reflected in the Buddha's mirror, they are evil. In fact, the Buddha sees humans as incapable of good.

By now the reader should have a clearer understanding of the Buddha's view of humankind.

The Evil That We Do Causes Us to Suffer in This Life and Again in the Life to Come

As soon as the wisteria vine he is clinging to breaks, the traveler must fall into the raging waters of a bottomless sea: this is the Buddha's warning. What is the deep sea that the Buddha speaks of here? As explained previously, it is the product of our three toxic worldly passions. The Buddha taught that because the bottomless sea issues from our own desire, anger, and ignorance, we must fall into it; the sea is, in fact, hell.

> The evildoer, committing evil, enters from suffering into suffering
>
> (Larger Sutra of Infinite Life)

The above words of the Buddha mean that as a result of the evil they commit, evil people suffer in this world, and, after dying, they suffer again in hell.

What are the torments of hell like? The Buddha told stories to help us imagine.

One day the Buddha saw a young woman standing on a big bridge, surreptitiously filling her pockets with stones. Realizing that she was about to kill herself, he rushed to her side and asked her solicitously what the matter was. When she saw who he was, she opened her heart and told him everything.

"I fell in love with a certain man, and afterward he abandoned me. Society is harsh, and I could see no future for the child in my womb. I decided in agony that we would both be better off dead. Please let me die." She broke down in tears.

Full of pity, the Buddha told her, "Listen to me. I have a story for you.

96   Chapter 2-9   The Raging Waters of a Bottomless Sea

Once there was an ox who had to pull a heavily laden cart every day from morning to night. The ox thought, 'Why must I suffer like this day after day? If it weren't for this cart, I wouldn't have to suffer so.' And so the ox decided to destroy the cart. He took off at a furious pace and dashed the cart against a huge rock, smashing it to pieces.

"The owner of the ox was astonished and said to himself, 'This ox has such a wild streak; I'd better use a sturdier cart, or the same thing will happen again.' He replaced the old cart with a new one made of steel, many times heavier than before. Once again, the ox had to work day after day pulling heavy loads in the new, heavy cart. His suffering was far greater than before. He deeply regretted what he had done, but it was too late.

"Like the ox who thought he could end his suffering by destroying the cart, you think you can find relief from your suffering by destroying your body. But although you don't know it, after you die, the suffering you experience in the next world will be many times greater than what you are going through now."

What the Buddha said to the suicidal young woman applies to each of us as well. Every creature that is born must also die, so the world beyond death—the afterlife—concerns us all. Throughout his life on earth, the Buddha taught rigorously about "the crucial matter of the afterlife." What will happen to us after we die?

The Torments of Hell Are Beyond the Power of Words to Describe

The Buddha made it plain that once the wisteria vine broke, the traveler was doomed to fall into the raging waters of a bottomless sea. The sea represents hell, where suffering is far greater than in this world. According to the Buddha, the torments of hell are beyond the power of words to describe. To help his disciples understand, he gave them an analogy.

"Imagine being pierced by one hundred lances every morning, noon, and night. What would that be like?" he asked.

"Being pierced by even one lance is painful. The agony of three hundred lances a day is unimaginable."

The Buddha then picked up a stone the size of his fist and asked a seemingly absurd question: "Which is bigger, this stone or the Himalayas off in the distance?"

"There is no comparison! They are in a completely different class from each other."

"If the suffering of being pierced by three hundred lances a day is this stone," said the Buddha, "then the suffering of hell is the Himalayas."

Explaining the actual torments of hell to people in this life is more impossible than explaining the workings of a computer to a dog or a cat.

What Comes After Death Is Beyond Human Comprehension

In the past, most people may have taken the concept of hell seriously, but today many people regard it derisively as a fairy tale. Such an opinion calls to mind this imaginary conversation among eels in the fish tank of a Japanese restaurant:

◆　◆　◆

"Quite a bustling place."

"That's because this is the Midsummer Day of the Ox. It's traditional for humans to eat us on this day."

"What? You're saying there are horrible eel-eating monsters called humans? I don't believe it."

"Whether you believe it or not, they're going to eat us."

"Did somebody come back after leaving this tank and tell you that?"

"Look, now another one of us has been captured and taken off somewhere."

"I bet he just went for a walk. He'll be back pretty soon."

"Getting captured means getting a stake pounded in your head, being sliced open and chopped in three, then skewered and roasted over an open flame. Yelling and cursing is useless since they don't speak our language. The cook is a demon, and so are the ones eating. They slice us in pieces and devour us, so none of us is coming back."

◆　◆　◆

Of course, there is a vast difference between eels and humans, but in any case, what comes after death is totally beyond human comprehension. Of course, that doesn't stop people from forming strong opinions:

"After we die, we're tortured by demons in hell, you say? Utter nonsense. Demons don't scare me. Bring 'em on! I'll crush 'em to death. Has anybody ever been to hell and back and told about it? When you die, your body turns to ashes, and your soul goes up in smoke—that's all. Don't waste your time worrying about stupid stuff. Drink up and enjoy life. That's all you need to do."

"Worry about it when you die; that's soon enough. Hardly anybody goes to the good place, so the path'll be overgrown with weeds, but lots of people go to the bad place, so the path won't have any weeds. Pick the weedy path, and you'll make it to paradise all right."

"I won't be the only one in hell. I'll have plenty of company, so it'll be jolly there."

But if an ocean liner went down and many people drowned, would that make it all right for you to drown too? This world is full of suffering. People are swept away in tsunamis or burn to death; they lose a beloved spouse or an only child; they go bankrupt. Does the presence of so many fellow sufferers make this world a jolly place?

People who look on death as something that happens only to other people may say they hold it in no fear, but when someone close to them dies suddenly, they change their tune: "Where has she gone? Will I never see her again? Where do we come from, and where do we go?" These fundamental questions regarding human life then arise.

Cicadas spend most of their lives underground, emerging finally for a few weeks in the summer. "The cicada knows nothing of spring or autumn," goes a Japanese proverb. The mind of a cicada cannot comprehend the seasons, but the mind of a human being can. Our minds cannot, however, fathom what comes after death. Whether there is an afterlife and, if there is, what it may be like are unknowable to us.

But all this was clearly revealed to the Buddha, who possessed the highest form of wisdom there is: the wisdom of a buddha.

Once the Buddha's disciples commented, "Since you have attained the enlightenment of a buddha, you must experience no suffering whatever."

"I do not experience distress as you do, but one thing does cause me grief. That is the sight of people falling like drops of rain into hell, deaf to all I tell them about the crucial matter of the afterlife, even though the torments of hell draw closer by the second. This is what makes me suffer."

The average Japanese person today dismisses talk of hell, associating it with demons in tiger-skin loincloths presiding over bubbling cauldrons. They laugh it off because they know nothing of the hell the Buddha referred to in his talks. That hell is a world of fierce, inconceivable suffering. The Sanskrit word for it is *naraka*. This was translated into Chinese as *diyu*, pronounced *jigoku* in Japanese. The word is widely used in secular contexts in Japan today. People speak of *shakkin jigoku*, "debt hell," for example, and refer to a dire situation as *abikyokan jigoku*, combining the names of two hot hells of Buddhism. Hell is not some far-off place; the word refers rather to a condition of intense and merciless suffering. Buddha taught that hell exists both in the present world and in the world to come, after we die.

Then, we may ask, what brings hell into existence? One old verse lays the answer bare.

> There is no carpenter
> that builds the burning carriage;
> it is you who builds it
> and you who rides it.

Ordinarily, a wooden carriage would be constructed by a carpenter, but the allegorical "burning carriage" mentioned here is built by none other than ourselves. We are the ones who make it, climb into it, and suffer as the fire burns our flesh. In other words, it is the evil deeds that we ourselves do that create hell for us, in accordance with the law of cause and effect. We are the ones who conjure our very own hell and bring agony upon ourselves. We think of hell as being a place that already exists somewhere, but it is actually a state that is brought forth by our own evil deeds.

The Buddha taught, "One's own karma, one's own takings." *One's own karma* means our own deeds, and *one's own takings* means our own results. Therefore, what this tells us is that all results that come to us are brought about by our own actions.

A common expression for this in English is "You reap what you sow." If someone who leads a disorderly life falls ill as a result, they are "reaping what they sowed"; the same is true of students who fail their exams because they chose to have fun instead of study.

The Buddha taught that all results that we experience are born of our own deeds without a single exception. We only ever reap what we ourselves have sown.

This is why, in the Buddha's analogy, the raging waters of the bottomless sea are produced by the three poisonous dragons; hell is the creation of the three toxic worldly passions of greed, anger, and ignorance.

10

Drops of Honey

Above the traveler's head, the tiger watches for a chance to attack. In the raging sea below the traveler's feet, three dragons wait for him to tumble into their gaping, bright-red mouths. A white mouse and a black mouse circle the top of the vine, each gnawing at it in turn. Eventually, one or the other of them will bite through.

Caught in this dreadful bind, what thoughts go through the traveler's head? What does he ponder?

All human emotions, even sheer terror and a sense of urgency, fade over time. The traveler begins to resign himself to his fate, figuring there is no point in struggling, but the activity of the two mice demands an instant response. Desperate to protect his lifeline, the traveler focuses all his efforts on driving the mice away. He shakes the vine as hard as he can, but the pace of the mice's gnawing never changes. Instead, with every movement of the vine, something drips down around him. He holds out a tentative hand and discovers it is honey. There is a hive at the top of the vine, and he rocked it so hard that drops of honey began to spill from the honeycomb.

The Mysterious Power Exerted by Five Kinds of Desire: Desire for Food, for Wealth, for Sexual Love, for Fame, and for Sleep

When the famished traveler licks the honey, it tastes so good that his insides melt, and he swoons. Captivated physically and mentally by the honey, he forgets all about the imminent danger he is in. One thought only occupies his mind: How can I get more honey to fall so that I can go on eating it? Truly, the drops of honey hold a kind of magical power to distract him. What do they signify? The Buddha explained that they represent the human desire for food, wealth, love, fame, and sleep.

The desire for food means the desire to satisfy one's hunger and thirst and to do so with as much pleasure as possible. Many travel enthusiasts find the joy of getting about lies less in sightseeing and more in trying new and delicious foods. Some people even go so far as to say, "If I could eat and drink whatever my heart desired, I'd die happy."

Second is the desire to increase one's money and possessions. Eager to make more money, we perk up at get-rich-quick schemes and follow tips on managing assets, reducing taxes, and the like. Our desire for wealth is reflected in our smile of satisfaction on seeing the balance in our savings account climb. It is why the purchase of a new home, a new car, or even a new pair of shoes gladdens the heart.

The desire for sexual love refers to the desire for an intimate romantic relationship with someone special. Since ancient times, courtship and romantic entanglements, including adulterous affairs and love triangles, have engendered countless incidents of enormous cruelty as love and hate intertwine and bitter accusations fly back and forth. Beneath it all is the longing to be with the man or woman you desire. The desire for sexual love keeps the mind in a constant whirl, obsessed with thoughts of the beloved.

Fourth, the desire for fame is the desire to be praised and appreciated. This is the mind that exults on winning a competition, coming in first in a tournament, or receiving some other form of public commendation. A student who passes a difficult examination and is told "Awesome!" or an office worker congratulated on a promotion will surely be wreathed in smiles.

Last is the desire for sleep, which refers not only to sleepiness but to indolence, the desire to take things easy and avoid hassles. Sometimes after the alarm goes off in the morning, we snuggle under the covers, loath to get out of bed. The desire for ease has led to the invention and continuous improvement of household appliances that make cooking, dishwashing, cleaning, and doing laundry far less laborious than in the past.

When you think about it, politics, economics, science, medicine, and all other fields of endeavor are aimed at satisfying these five desires of humanity. In the Buddha's parable, the traveler, who represents us all, thinks only of how to live in order to obtain more honey for himself, which is to say to satisfy the five desires. The Buddha strongly urges us to reflect upon our actions.

Though the Buddha Spoke Throughout His Life About the Crucial Matter of the Afterlife, Few Believed Him

The parable "The True Nature of Human Existence" is of course not a categorical denial of the pleasure of satisfying the five desires. It is rather the Buddha's solemn warning to humanity. Each of us is a traveler dangling from a slender wisteria vine above a churning, bottomless sea, while overhead a white mouse and a black mouse circle the vine, each gnawing on it in turn—yet our minds remain focused on drops of honey. The Buddha wants to impress upon us the horrific peril we are in.

> People of this world are shallow and vulgar, struggling over things of no urgency.
>
> (Larger Sutra of Infinite Life)

Like all people, we are transfixed by the honey in front of our noses and know nothing of the crucial matter of the afterlife. When the wisteria vine breaks, we fear the bottomless sea we are falling toward and regret having cared only about honey, but it is too late.

> As life ends, regret and fear occur by turns.
>> (Larger Sutra of Infinite Life)

The Buddha is sounding the alarm. Humans dangle from a vine, thinking only of honey, even though at any moment a mouse will gnaw through the vine and send them plummeting to the angry sea below: this impending doom is what the Buddha calls "the crucial matter of the afterlife."

> Few believe, even if they are taught and exhorted. Birth-and-death continues without cease, and the path of evil never ends.
>> (Larger Sutra of Infinite Life)

Here the Buddha is lamenting: "No matter how patiently I teach the crucial matter of the afterlife, few believe me; hardly anyone has had their suffering eliminated and been granted true happiness." His heart is filled with sorrow and concern.

CHAPTER 3

There Is a Light That Destroys
the Darkness of Despair

How Can the Traveler Clinging to a Slender Vine, Preoccupied by Honey, Be Saved?

The reader may have gained the impression that this parable by the Buddha offers no hope of salvation. But the Buddha did not lay out the stark truth of humanity's plight in order to push us into an abyss of despair. Rather, he did it out of urgent necessity, the way a physician treating a critically ill patient carefully explains her diagnosis in order to gain the patient's understanding and cooperation. She also gives detailed explanations of medications and treatment. No physician would simply make a broad diagnosis and stop there. In the same way, the Buddha describes our true plight in stark terms and carefully explains the crucial matter of the afterlife precisely because he knows the remedy. Throughout his life, he devoted himself to the grand purpose of his appearance in this world: to show all people how to resolve the crucial matter of the afterlife here and now, in this life, and attain supreme happiness.

What can save a traveler who is hanging from a slender vine about to break with no thought in his mind but drops of honey?

The Larger Sutra of Infinite Life, where the Buddha sets forth the purpose of his appearance on earth, presents the answer concisely with absolute certainty: "*Ikko sennen muryoju butsu.*" (Believe single-mindedly in the Buddha of Infinite Life.) Nearly two millennia later, Shinran, the founder of the True Pure Land School of Buddhism in Japan, declared this to be the most important teaching in Buddhism, the conclusion to which everything the Buddha preached leads.

What exactly is the Buddha urging us to do? Here is a paraphrase: "Focus your mind only on the Buddha of Infinite Life, and offer him and him alone your utmost devotion."

What sort of buddha is the Buddha of Infinite Life? This name refers to Amida Buddha, the master buddha. The historical Buddha of whom we have been speaking, whose name is Śākyamuni, must not be confused with Amida Buddha. Śākyamuni, who was born in Lumbini 2,600 years ago and is the only person on earth ever to have attained the enlightenment of a buddha, always said "Amida Buddha is my master" and held Amida in highest respect.

Śākyamuni also said, "There are countless worlds like Earth in the universe, and so, just as I was born on this planet, there are other buddhas elsewhere, on countless other worlds. Amida Buddha is the master of us all." Śākyamuni Buddha and all the other buddhas are disciples of Amida, and he is their teacher.

In his sutras, Śākyamuni quotes the mass of buddhas singing Amida's praise:

> Amida Buddha is the king among all the buddhas. (Great Amida Sutra)

> Amida's light is king of all buddhas' lights; among them it is supreme.
> (Sutra of Equal Enlightenment)

Not only Śākyamuni Buddha but all the buddhas of the universe look up to Amida Buddha as their teacher. There is, of course, a reason for this: Amida possesses great virtue—virtue lacking in all other buddhas. He has a great many names referring to that superior virtue, including the most famous one: the Buddha of Infinite Life. Therefore, the exhortation to offer single-minded devotion to the Buddha of Infinite Life means to focus one's whole mind on Amida Buddha alone with utmost devotion.

Saving the traveler who is besotted by drops of honey while hanging from a vine about to snap is an impossible task, one far beyond the power of Śākyamuni Buddha or even the combined power of all the buddhas in the ten directions. Cast aside by all buddhas, the traveler is doomed to fall into the angry sea and be consumed by three poisonous dragons. Salvation can come only from Amida Buddha, so turn to Amida alone with utmost devotion. This was Śākyamuni Buddha's lifelong message.

Amida Saves Us into Absolute Happiness in This Life and Makes Us Set to Go to the Pure Land

Amida knows human nature—represented in the allegory by the traveler—full well. He carefully observed humanity's plight and saw beyond any doubt that saving the foolish, sinful human race was beyond the powers of all the buddhas in the universe. "I alone will save you," he said and made his peerless vow, the famous Primal Vow of Amida Buddha.

Amida Buddha vowed, "I will save anyone at all in this life, resolve their crucial matter of the afterlife, and grant them absolute happiness in an *ichinen*, making them set to go to the Pure Land without fail." An *ichinen* is the smallest possible unit of time.

Human promises sometimes are broken, but Amida's Vow can never be broken. Amida swore that if he could not fulfill his Vow, he would cease to be a buddha. And he created the six-character *Myogo* (Name) *Namu Amida Butsu*, which has the power to fulfill his Vow.

The monk Rennyo wrote:

> *"Namu Amida Butsu"* is written with only six Chinese characters, so it seems unlikely to possess any great virtue. Yet the virtue that lies within this six-character Name is supreme and profound, without limit.　　(*The Letters,* 5:13)

The virtue within *Namu Amida Butsu*, which Rennyo describes as "supreme and profound, without limit," is the twofold virtue of destroying darkness and fulfilling Amida's Vow. In destroying darkness, *Namu Amida Butsu* imparts vast security. In fulfilling Amida's Vow, it imparts complete satisfaction. The anxiety of the traveler clinging to a vine that he knows may snap at any moment is relieved, and he has the great security of knowing with assurance that when the vine does snap, he will fall into Amida's Pure Land.

This is why, even though humankind is hanging from a slender vine, so besotted with drops of honey that they cannot think of anything else, the Buddha devoted his life to preaching Amida's Vow, the true purpose of his coming into the world.

122   Chapter 3   There Is a Light That Destroys the Darkness of Despair

> I came into this world … to bless all people with
> salvation through the Vow of Amida Buddha.
>> (Larger Sutra of Infinite Life)

Here Śākyamuni Buddha declares that he was born on this planet to preach Amida's Vow and guide all people into absolute happiness.

Shinran expressed his gratitude and joy in this hymn:

> Śākyamuni and Amida,
> our compassionate father and mother,
> with various marvelous expedients
> cause peerless faith to rise within us.[3]

What exactly is Amida's Vow? How can we be saved into absolute happiness? These are the questions that the Buddha addressed and explained throughout his eighty years of life.

3 *Hymns on the Masters.*

To Be Born Human Is a Rare and Precious Thing

Through his precious teaching, Śākyamuni continues even now to speak to us as we stand before the gate of Buddhism.

> Human form is difficult to obtain; now I have already obtained it.
> Buddhist truth is difficult to hear; now I have already heard it.

With the words "human form is difficult to obtain," he is urging all people to realize the significance of having been born human. Do we not think little of having been born human? During life's trials, do we not resent or regret having been born? This is a terrible waste. To be born human is a rare and precious thing, he assures us.

Once Śākyamuni asked his disciple Ānanda, "What do you think about having been born human?"

"I feel extremely fortunate," replied Ānanda, whereupon the Buddha told the following story:

"At the bottom of a vast ocean there was a blind turtle. Once every hundred years, the turtle poked its head out of the water. Floating on the surface of the ocean was a log, and in the middle of the log was a hole. The log drifted with the wind in all directions. Tell me, Ānanda. What were the chances that when that blind turtle came up, its head would go into the hole in the log?"

"Master, such a thing could hardly happen!"

"Are you saying that it could never happen?" the Buddha asked.

"Well, in a billion or trillion years, there may be a chance, but it is so unlikely, one could call it impossible."

"Ānanda, to be born human is still more difficult than for that turtle to poke its head through the hole in the log. Human life is truly rare and precious."

That parable is found in the Miscellaneous Agama Sutra. The Nirvana Sutra contains this stunning statement by the Buddha:

> Those born human are like sand on a fingernail.
> Those who fall into the three realms of suffering
> are like sands in the ten directions.

The *three realms of suffering* refers to the realms of most intense suffering: hell, the realm of hungry ghosts, and the realm of animals. While those born human are as few as the grains of sand on a fingernail, those who fall into the three realms of suffering are as many as the grains of sand in the universe. Of the three, the only one we are capable of imagining is the realm of animals, which includes insects and other life forms. At present, there are some 1.75 million different kinds of known animals on this earth. Including unknown species could bring the total to over thirty million. Ants alone vastly outnumber human beings; scientists believe there are over two million times as many ants on earth as there are people.

In this way, the rarity of being born human is amply demonstrated by comparison with the realm of animals alone. Śākyamuni taught that even more beings are suffering in hell and the realm of hungry ghosts. To receive life in the human realm is indeed exceedingly rare.

"Human form is difficult to obtain": obtaining human form is our first hurdle in establishing a bond with Buddhism.

This Life Is Our Chance to Escape the Realms of Suffering

Now let us consider the meaning of "Buddhist truth is difficult to hear; now I have already heard it."

Buddhist truth is "difficult to hear" because without bonds from previous lives, the desire to listen to Amida's Vow could not be raised within you, and without that desire, listening to Buddhist truth (Amida's Vow) would be quite impossible.

To illustrate the wonder of being blessed with the desire to listen to Amida's Vow, Śākyamuni made this comparison: "It is more difficult than dropping a thread from a Himalayan peak and threading it through the eye of a needle at the foot of the mountain." Threading a needle is hard enough when you hold it in your hand. Doing so from the summit of a mountain more than 26,000 feet high would certainly be impossible.

Sadly, the world is full of people who, despite the precious gift of life in the human realm, lack any bond with Buddhism. Even those who claim to profess the Buddha's teachings merely point to one part and announce, "This is what Buddhism is." Those who correctly teach Amida's Vow, the very reason for the Buddha's appearance in this world, are fewer than stars on a rainy night. Each time we see or hear reminders of this terrible state of affairs, the meaning of the teaching that "Buddhist truth is difficult to hear" sinks deeper into the heart.

The difficulty of hearing Buddhist truth is indeed the second hurdle in establishing a bond with Buddhism. Any reader who has come this far in this book, listening to the teachings of Buddha (Amida's Vow) that are so "difficult to hear," surely has deep ties with Buddhism.

To all those who have surmounted the hurdles and established a bond with Buddhism, Śākyamuni offers his blessing and encouragement:

If you do not achieve salvation in this lifetime,
when will you ever do so?

If you are not saved in this life, when against all odds you have been born into the human realm, in what realm will you find salvation? This is your only chance. These are Śākyamuni's precious words, urging us with all his might to seize this chance to leave the realms of suffering once and for all.

Some who read the Buddha's encouragement may still feel like giving up, fearing it is too late for them. But Amida's Vow saves one and all into absolute happiness through hearing alone, without regard for age or ability.

Śākyamuni's words of encouragement concerning Amida's salvation are clear and ringing:

> All sentient beings,
> in the *ichinen* of hearing that Name (*Myogo*),
> will gain true faith and great joy.
> (Larger Sutra of Infinite Life)

The Buddha is kindly explaining that in the *ichinen* of hearing and receiving Amida's creation, *Namu Amida Butsu*, anyone at all can attain absolute happiness. An *ichinen* is a unit of time shorter than one second, so even those on their deathbeds can be saved and go to the Pure Land when they die, as the Buddha asserted. Since Amida's salvation takes place in an *ichinen*, it is never too late.

This is why the single focus of Śākyamuni's teaching is urging everyone to listen to Amida's Vow.

Achieving Eternal Happiness in This Life Is the Sole Purpose for Which We Were Born Human

We would like to conclude with a famous episode said to have occurred at Śākyamuni's birth, with deep significance regarding the purpose of being born human.

As soon as he was born, the future buddha took seven steps in each of the four directions, north, south, east, and west. Then he pointed to the sky with his right hand and the earth with his left and said, "In heaven and earth, I have one sacred mission."

It's hard to imagine that a newborn infant could walk and talk, future buddha or not, but the incident is recorded in the sutras as a topic that sheds light on Śākyamuni's lifelong teachings. First, the seven steps he took in each of the four directions have profound significance. Throughout his life, Śākyamuni taught that the realms of endless suffering are six in all: first, the three realms of most intense suffering—which, as we've seen, are hell, the realm of hungry ghosts, and the realm of animals—and then three further realms, which are the realm of asuras, the realm of human beings, and the realm of celestial beings. Together these are called the *six realms of delusion*. According to Śākyamuni, our eternal self has been caught in the endless cycle of birth and death, always suffering. This is known as *transmigration in the six realms.*

Since our ultimate purpose in being born human is to escape the suffering of this endless circle of transmigration through the six realms, the symbolism of the infant Buddha's seventh step is highly meaningful.

What about the words spoken by the infant Buddha? What do they mean? The utterance consists of two phrases. The first, "in heaven and earth," refers to the vastness of the universe. The second is widely misinterpreted to mean something like "I alone am sacred." The actual meaning is completely different. Anyone truly noble and virtuous is humble and respectful; as the proverb goes, "The mature rice plant lowers its head." The Buddha, of all people, would never make an arrogant declaration. The pronoun *I* means not only Śākyamuni Buddha, but every single individual without exception. The meaning of the second phrase thus becomes, "We humans are born into this world with a single sacred mission to perform." This is a truly unprecedented declaration.

What then is our single sacred mission in this life? None other than to listen to Amida's Vow, be saved into absolute happiness, and escape forever from the six realms of delusion. The message is one of encouragement, because only those born in the realm of human beings can listen to Amida's Vow and achieve the purpose of life. Śākyamuni's lifelong message was, "Hear and believe Amida's Vow, and attain absolute happiness from this life on. This is the sole purpose of being born human."

What is it like, the world of absolute happiness we attain once we are saved by Amida's Vow? The Buddha likened it to an ocean, the vast home into which all rivers flow. Raindrops that fall on mountain peaks trickle steadily on, perhaps pausing along the way in a reservoir or lake but always flowing into the ocean in the end. In the same way, everyone's lives are full of twists and turns, but listen and be saved by Amida's Vow, and you, too, will enter the vast ocean of brightness without fail. Even now, Śākyamuni continues his appeal.

When the water of many rivers enters the sea, it all becomes one in flavor, and in the same way, everyone who is saved by Amida's Vow attains equal happiness, without any distinction of race, wealth, or ability.

What must I do to enter that ocean? You may be asking yourself this with some anxiety. But anyone who has read this book carefully is like a raindrop that has fallen on the seashore: the great ocean of absolute happiness lies right before you, well within your reach.

Everyone can look back on their life and recall many ups and downs and memorable events. We all have experienced pleasant times when we smiled to ourselves with delight. We also have known plenty of pain and suffering, times when we were plunged into the depths of despair. Sometimes we endure and finally overcome our troubles. Other times we reflect on our experiences with regret and wonder what the meaning of our suffering could be. But every bit of our lives is a part of the process of fulfilling our one purpose in having been born human. Not one moment is wasted, the Buddha assures us, as he watches over us with tenderness.

This very moment, each one of us is the star of our own story, advancing surely toward the great path of no hindrance, lit by Amida's infinite light.

AFTERWORD

Who Was the Buddha?

Śākyamuni Buddha was born some 2,600 years ago as the firstborn son of King Suddhodana and Queen Mahāmāyā, who lived in Kapilavastu Palace in India. His given name was Siddhārtha.

The prince was extraordinarily bright. He studied under the finest scholars and masters of military arts, but in a famous episode, they resigned en masse, declaring they had no more to teach him. Contemplative and levelheaded even as a boy, the prince one day watched a bird eat an insect and so discovered the law of the jungle: the strong prey on the weak; life requires the sacrifice of other life. The harshness of this reality caused the prince great pain.

He Sought Happiness Transcending Aging, Sickness, and Death

One day, after the prince had grown up, he decided to step outside Kapilavastu Palace, his home. First he went out the East Gate and was astonished to see an old man with a wrinkled face, bent back, and shaking hands hobbling along on a cane. "Everyone, even those who are now young, will grow old, ugly, and decrepit and be treated as a nuisance." This revelation made him disconsolate.

Next he went out the West Gate and saw someone sick, his face screwed up in a painful cough, struggling for breath. This brought another shock: "Today's health is only temporary; illness can strike at any time."

When Siddhārtha went out the South Gate, he encountered a funeral procession and saw with his own eyes the motionless body of the deceased. "People fawn over me now, but even I will have to die one day."

Finally, he went out the North Gate and was moved by the sight of an ascetic. The prince felt strongly that seeking a happiness that transcended aging, sickness, and death was the path he needed to take.

These famous events are known as Prince Siddhārtha's "excursions out of the four gates." Through these experiences, he came face to face for the first time with old age, sickness, and death. He understood that blessings of health, status, honor, ability, and wealth must in time be canceled by these three. No happiness lasts forever. Knowing this, he could no longer feel secure or satisfied.

One night, the prince awoke in the middle of the night and saw beautiful court ladies who had adorned themselves and danced for him that afternoon lying sprawled in sleep, disheveled and wanton in appearance, without a trace of their previous elegant, modest loveliness. He was appalled to realize he had been deceived by mere surface charm. All kinds of pleasure and entertainment, he now realized, were no more than a temporary distraction, a form of deception. He resolved on the spot to leave the palace and forthwith set off for the mountains to become an ascetic. He was twenty-nine years old.

For the next six years, the prince subjected himself to austerities no one had ever attempted before. Finally, sitting under a bodhi tree, he attained the highest level of enlightenment, the enlightenment of a buddha.

There are many different levels of enlightenment in Buddhism, fifty-two in all, each with its own name. This is similar to the world of sumo wrestling, for example, where wrestlers enter in the lowest division, *jonokuchi*, and gradually work their way up to the highest division, *makunouchi*, which has five ranks ending in *ozeki* (champion) and *yokozuna* (grand champion). The highest level of Buddhist enlightenment is known as *supreme enlightenment* or *the enlightenment of a buddha*. Only those who have attained this enlightenment can be called Buddha.

Attaining supreme enlightenment means reaching the truth that leads to happiness. This truth differs from scientific truths such as "water is formed of hydrogen and oxygen" or mathematical truths such as "1 + 1 = 2." *Truth* in Buddhism means the ultimate truth whereby all people can gain absolute happiness.

As a mountain climber reaches steadily higher elevations, the surrounding view opens up more and more, until at the top of the mountain the view is unrestricted in all directions. In the same way, only those who have reached the highest stage of enlightenment can apprehend the full truth whereby everlasting happiness is made available to all people.

A vast number of people have been born and died on this earth, and of them all, only Śākyamuni Buddha has ever attained the highest level of enlightenment. This is why when people say *the Buddha*, they refer to him.

The difference between each level of enlightenment is said to be as great as the difference in wisdom between a human being and an insect. Recall the old Japanese saying, "A cicada knows nothing of spring or autumn." Cicadas live aboveground for only seven days in midsummer. To expect a cicada to understand spring and autumn, let alone winter and snow, is unreasonable.

Since each rung on the ladder of enlightenment represents a leap in wisdom equivalent to that between cicadas and human beings, the wisdom of the Buddha, at the fifty-second level, is exponentially greater than ours. Over two and a half millennia ago, he taught that the universe contains countless worlds similar to Earth. On a clear night, the sky is full of sparkling stars. Our planet is part of the solar system, revolving around the sun along with Mercury, Venus, Mars, Jupiter, and the rest. The Milky Way is a galaxy containing two hundred billion solar systems, and the cosmos contains more than one hundred billion galaxies in all. The Buddha called a system containing one thousand Earth-like worlds a *small chiliocosm* (equivalent to solar system); one thousand small chiliocosms he called a *medium chiliocosm* (equivalent to galaxy); and one thousand medium chiliocosms he called a *great chiliocosm* (equivalent to galaxy cluster). The totality of these systems he called the *trichiliocosm*, or universe.

When Copernicus proposed the heliocentric theory of the universe in 1543, people still believed that the sun revolved around the Earth and the Earth was the center of the universe. It is amazing to think that more than two millennia before Copernicus, Śākyamuni taught this far-reaching view of the cosmos, using terminology roughly equivalent to that used by astronomers today.

◆ ◆ ◆

Sutras Are the Buddha's Collected Sermons

To convey the truth made known to him through the wisdom he gained upon attaining supreme enlightenment, for forty-five years—from his enlightenment at thirty-five to his death at eighty—Śākyamuni Buddha preached a great many sermons all around India. His disciples recorded his sermons and collected them in what are known as *sutras*. They include the Larger Sutra of Infinite Life, the Lotus Sutra, the Nirvana Sutra, and many more. In all there are some seven thousand volumes containing his lifelong teachings.

The frontispiece of this book illustrates content from the Parable Sutra.

COLUMN

One summer day, a cicada landed on a plum tree and noticed that the plums growing there differed in size and shape. Some were large, others small; some were round, others flattened. The cicada was puzzled and muttered, "This makes no sense."

We might try to explain: "You crawled out of the ground in June, so all you know is summer. While you were underground, back in what's called spring, this tree was covered in white blossoms. Some were visited by bees and butterflies, and others were not, causing discrepancy in the size of the plums." Despite our best efforts, the cicada would only scoff and fail to understand.

Unlike humans, a cicada lacks the necessary experience to grasp the concepts of spring and fall. In just the same way, while the Buddha possesses the wisdom that is needed to fully comprehend the three temporal worlds of the past, present, and future, human beings do not. The three worlds are as far beyond our understanding as the different seasons are for a cicada.

POSTSCRIPT

Living on the Path of No Hindrance

Life's Purpose and *Tannisho*

Tannisho (Lamenting the Deviations) is a beloved classic, widely read and highly esteemed, but few know the book's real message. In it, Shinran teaches that the ultimate purpose of life is to gain true happiness and live on a path free from all hindrances. Before one who has been brought onto that path, he says, "Gods of heaven and earth bow their heads in reverence, and evil spirits and false teachings can pose no obstacle." A detailed explanation can be found in my book *Unlocking Tannisho: Shinran's Words on the Pure Land Path*.

Kentetsu Takamori

BIBLIOGRAPHY

Eto, Jun, *Tsuma to watashi* [My Wife and I], *Bungei shunju*, May 1999, 94–133.

Kishimoto, Hideo, *Shi o mitsumeru kokoro – Gan to tatakatta junenkan* [The Mind Trained on Death:

Ten Years Fighting Cancer] (Tokyo: Kodansha, 1973), 16–17.

Rennyo, *Gobunsho* [The Letters], in *Shinshu shiryo shusei*, ed. Osamu Katata, vol. 2 (Kyoto:

Dohosha, 1977).

Tillich, Paul, *The Courage to Be* (New Haven and London: Yale University Press, 2000).

Tolstoy, Leo, "A Confession," in *A Confession and Other Religious Writings*, trans. Jane Kentish

(London: Penguin Books Ltd., 1987).

Author
Kentetsu Takamori

Born in Toyama Prefecture, Japan, in 1929, he graduated from Ryukoku University in Kyoto.

Takamori has lectured widely in Japan and overseas and is the author of *Unlocking Tannisho: Shinran's Words on the Pure Land Path, Unshakable Spirit: Stories of Compassion and Wisdom*, and many other works.

Translator
Juliet Winters Carpenter

Born in Michigan in 1948, she is professor emerita of Doshisha Women's College of Liberal Arts and has won numerous awards for her translations, including the 2021-2022 Lindsey and Masao Miyoshi Translation Prize for lifetime achievement as a translator of modern Japanese literature. She has translated many books by Kentetsu Takamori, including *Unlocking Tannisho: Shinran's Words on the Pure Land Path*.

Illustrator

Hidekichi Shigemoto

Born in Ehime Prefecture, Japan, in 1956, Shigemoto graduated from the Design Department of Osaka University of Arts, where he is currently a visiting professor. After working as a designer and a freelance illustrator, he became a *sumi-e* artist. His innovative ink drawings of musicians, athletes, and other human figures, combining the traditional material of black *sumi* ink with his signature touch of speed and dynamism, have attracted attention both in Japan and overseas. He also gives live performances at solo exhibitions and other events, completing multiple large *sumi-e* simultaneously in a short space of time.